ULTIMATE SURVIVAL GUIDE FOR KIDS

QED

Copyright © Marshall Editions
2014
First published in the UK in
2014 by
QED Publishing
A Quarto Group company
The Old Brewery
6 Blundell Street
London N7 9BH
www.qed-publishing.co.uk

ISBN 978-1-78171-680-9

A catalogue record for this
book is available from the
British Library.

Produced for Marshall
Editions by Tall Tree Ltd
Illustrations by Tom Connell

Printed and bound in China
(September 2014-118641)

DISCLAIMER:
You should NEVER
put yourself in
dangerous situations
to test whether this
advice really works.
The publisher
cannot accept
responsibility for
any injuries, damage,
loss or prosecutions
resulting from
the information
in this book.

CONTENTS

Hopefully you will never face any of the extreme dangers described in the first part of this book. But if you do, here are some ideas about how best to survive. In the final chapter, you'll find practical advice for situations you could face when you set off on your adventures.

ANIMAL DANGERS

In our homes, animals are cute, cuddly companions. But out in the wild, they can be dangerous enemies and potential predators.

In snake country, always wear long trousers, thick socks and boots

WHAT TO DO IF YOU ARE BITTEN BY A SNAKE

Snakes rarely eat people. They don't attack because they are hungry, but because they are frightened or have been provoked.

DID YOU KNOW?
Snakes live all over the world, but especially in warm places such as deserts and rainforests.

Snakes smell using the tip of their forked tongue.

Wash the bite with soap and water. Keep it immobilized in a position lower than the heart to slow the flow of venom.

Never try to cut out or suck out the poison. Do not put anything cool, such as ice, on the bite.

Find a doctor. If you can't reach a doctor in 30 minutes, wrap a bandage tightly 8 cm above the bite.

There are around 2,700 species of snake, of which 375 are venomous. Snakes inject venom into their prey using two sharp fangs.

Snake bites can be treated using special medicine called antivenom. Venom is extracted (or milked) from snakes (shown right). This is then injected into an animal, which produces antibodies in its blood. The blood is then extracted to make the medicine.

Rattlesnakes shake their tails to warn potential predators.

▲ *Snake attack*

Around 1,500 people are bitten by snakes in Australia each year.

IF YOU
SEE A SNAKE

Stand very still. Don't go near it or try to touch it. And never try to prod it or kill it. Back away slowly and give it lots of room. Snakes can strike over half their body length in an instant.

The world's largest crocodiles can grow more than 7 m in length

OW TO ESCAPE FROM A CROCODILE

Most crocodiles and alligators rush away into the water if they see humans – unless they feel cornered or are defending their nest.

Covering a croc's eyes can calm it down

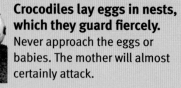

Crocodiles lay eggs in nests, which they guard fiercely. Never approach the eggs or babies. The mother will almost certainly attack.

Crocodiles can snap their jaws shut with enormous force. But the muscles controlling the opening of the jaws are much weaker. In fact, it's possible to keep a croc's jaws shut just using an elastic band.

LIFE SAVERS

 Try to hit the animal on the nose or in the eyes. Use a weapon if you can.

 If you are on land, try to get on the animal's back and push down on its neck. This will force its head down.

 If the animal has you in its jaws, try to keep its mouth clamped shut. This will stop it from shaking and wounding you.

Crocs hover at the water's surface looking for prey.

△*Each crocodile jaw has 24 sharp, crushing teeth.*

DID YOU KNOW?
Crocodiles and alligators are found in the slow-moving water of rivers, lakes and coastal mangrove swamps.

IF YOU SEE A CROC

Never approach it. Freeze and slowly back away.
Don't run. Crocodiles can move faster than you can. Never try to feed crocodiles, you may make them lose their fear of humans.

WHAT TO DO IF YOU SEE A SHARK

There are more than 370 types of shark, but very few of them are a danger to swimmers. Sharks that do attack usually live in warm waters.

If in the water, get out as fast as possible. Do not shout or splash – the shark may mistake you for a wounded animal.

If diving or surfing, don't lie at the surface. From below, you may look like a turtle or a seal, or other shark prey.

If on a boat, do not enter the water. Try scaring the shark with big actions. As a last resort, jab it on the nose with a paddle.

◁Sensors along the length of the shark's body detect vibrations in the water.

DID YOU KNOW?

People kill about 100 million sharks every year. Yet only about 100 people die each year in shark attacks.

Shark tooth – actual size

△ Sharks' teeth are serrated for tearing and slicing flesh.

IF YOU ARE ATTACKED

Try to punch or poke the shark hard in the eyes or gills. If you have equipment in your hands, use it as a weapon.
Keep hitting the shark. It may decide to give up the attack. If a shark bumps you in the water and then swims away, it may be preparing to attack. Get out of the water!

Sharks have an incredibly keen sense of smell.
They can detect a single drop of blood in a million drops of water, and they can smell blood in the sea from 0.4 km away.

Sharks have good eyesight.
Like cats, they have a mirror-like layer at the back of the eye, which doubles the amount of incoming light in dim water.

FAST FACTS

HOW TO ESCAPE FROM A BEAR

Bears live in mountains and forests. They are shy creatures, but also curious, so if you hike or camp in a forest, there is a chance you will see one.

A large bear may stand up to 3 m high

Bears can smell food from a long way away.
Wrap any food you have in a 'bear safe' container. If you are camping, never eat or keep any food in your tent – not even a bar of chocolate.

Bears are timid animals.
If you walk in a group and make lots of noise, they will be scared away. Never wander alone or hike at night.

LIFE SAVERS

▽ *Except during breeding times, bears remain solitary for most of the year.*

IF YOU ARE ATTACKED

Fall to the ground and roll into a ball. Play dead until the bear leaves you alone. If it attacks you at night in your tent, try to strike its eyes and nose. Make as much noise as you can.

 Do not make eye contact. Stand still, keep quiet and slowly back away. The bear will probably leave you alone.

 Never shout or run away. A bear can run much faster than you. If you climb a tree, a bear may climb up after you.

 If you are in a car, stay where you are. Never stop to take a photo. Do not get out of the car or open the windows.

H))W TO ESCAPE FROM A WILD CAT

Wild cats, such as tigers, live in forests, grasslands and mountains. They are shy, but will defend their territory if they feel threatened.

1 **Stay calm and face the animal.**
Make eye contact. Back slowly away and do not run. Pick up any younger children.

2 **Speak or growl in a loud voice.**
This will show that you are not prey and may possibly be a danger to the cat.

3 **If the cat follows, try to appear larger.**
Put your hands in the air and wave. Do not crouch – this makes you look like prey.

Wild cats are active after dusk.
Do not hike alone, especially at night. Carry a good hiking stick. It may come in useful to frighten or defend yourself from a cat.

While some wild cats search for prey, others lie in wait.
Keep a lookout for places where a cat might hide, such as rocks or low-lying bushes. Some wild cats, including tigers, jaguars and cheetahs, have excellent camouflage.

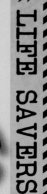

LIFE SAVERS

▽ *With lithe bodies, acute senses and sharp teeth and claws, tigers are superb hunters.*

IF YOU ARE ATTACKED
· · · · · · · · · · · · · · · ·

Without turning your back, throw branches and stones at the cat. Fight back aggressively to show that you're not prey – aim for the cat's eyes and mouth. Protect your neck. This is the area the cat will attack.

The Siberian tiger can leap 15 m

WHAT TO DO IF YOU ARE CHASED BY BEES

Bees are usually peaceful creatures, but if they feel threatened or under attack they can become extremely angry and may attack in swarms.

DID YOU KNOW?

Angry bees may continue to chase you for up to 150 m. That's longer than the length of a football field.

 1 Run away at once. Do not swat at the bees as this will make them even angrier and even more likely to attack.

 2 Seek shelter. If possible, head indoors or run through the thickest, bushiest foliage you can find.

 3 Don't submerge yourself in water. The bees may still be waiting for you when you surface.

A bees' nest may contain up to 60,000 bees

△Bees can fly at up to 32 km/h.

Bee hair – close up

IF YOU
ARE STUNG

Remove the sting gently by brushing it with your finger or pulling it with tweezers.
If you have trouble breathing, it may be an allergic reaction – get medical help immediately.

◁There are nearly 20,000 known species of bees.

Bees have a long proboscis (like a tongue).

Bees are social animals and live in large groups called colonies.

A bee nearly always dies when it stings a human. Its barbed sting gets caught in our skin and is ripped out of the bee's body.

A bee's sting is covered in tiny barbs.

Bees can sting other types of insect without losing their stings.

2,243 – that's the record number of stings suffered by one person who survived to tell the tale.

FAST FACTS

HOW TO ESCAPE FROM ANTS

Army ants march in long columns containing millions of ants. Raiding through a forest, they kill everything in their path.

▽ *A column of army ants can kill 100,000 insects and other creatures a day.*

1 **If you see an ant column, do not step on it.** You will break the ants' scent trail and they may run in all directions.

2 **Warn other people.** Lead any young children away from the area. Help the adults carry any babies in the group.

3 **Free any animals from ropes or pens.** Horses, goats and chickens could all be killed if attacked by army ants.

Jaws of an army ant

IF YOU ARE STUNG

Do not shake your legs in panic.

If alarmed, ants will produce a special chemical that will make other ants attack you. Run away fast. The best way to get rid of them is to jump in water, but make sure it is safe first.

DID YOU KNOW?
Army ants are almost always on the move. They eat all the food in one territory before moving on to the next.

An ant column can stretch for over 1 km

FAST FACTS

Army ants can form living bridges and ladders.
These ants swarm easily across any terrain. They join their bodies to descend drops or cross gaps in the ground.

Ants sting and bite.
The sharp jaws of army ants can kill animals that are tied up and unable to flee. Fire ants have a powerful sting that leaves itchy blisters.

A 'ladder' made entirely of army ants.

NATURAL DANGERS

Sometimes it can seem like the weather is out to get us. Hurricanes and earthquakes destroy cities, while forest fires and avalanches test even the toughest travellers.

HOW TO ESCAPE FROM QUICKSAND

Quicksand is soft, wet, sticky sand that is easy to sink into – and sometimes get stuck. It is found in areas where sand or clay have become severely waterlogged.

△ *The quicker you move, the faster you will sink.*

Most quicksand is just a few inches deep

Quickly warn anyone who is behind you to stop them falling in, too. You will probably need their help to get out.

Try to reach firm ground or grab something like a tuft of grass. You may be able to use this to pull yourself free.

Take off anything that might be weighing you down. This could include your backpack or a heavy jacket.

IF SOMEONE ELSE IS IN QUICKSAND

Tell the person to stay calm and move slowly. Get them to take off any heavy objects that might be weighing them down. Find a long stick or a branch. Lay down at the edge of the quicksand and hold out the branch so the person can grab it. Carefully pull them to safety.

Do not plunge in after them. You will only get trapped yourself.

FAST FACTS

Quicksand is found in wet areas, such as beaches, riverbanks and lake shorelines. It can also be found in marshes and near underground springs and mountain streams.

Places that are well known for having areas of quicksand usually have warning signs. Be sure to look out for them when you are walking.

You can use a branch to pull yourself, or a friend, out of quicksand if you get stuck.

4 **Try to remain calm. Do not panic. Don't thrash around.** The more you move, the faster the quicksand will pull you down.

5 **Lean backwards and spread your arms and legs to help you float.** Gently push yourself to firmer ground, taking the shortest route you can.

6 **If you have a stick with you, lean across it.** Then, move it crosswise under your hips where it will help to support you as you move.

OW TO SURVIVE A HURRICANE

Hurricanes are dangerous, swirling storms that bring high seas, huge waves, heavy rains and terrifying winds. They can cause a lot of damage.

▷ *Hurricanes are tropical storms with winds of more than 118 km/h.*

Help board up the windows and doors. If there is a risk of flooding, move valuable things upstairs.

If you live near the coast, you will be told to evacuate. Make sure your family allows enough time to do this.

Take your pets with you or lock them inside the house. Leave food and water. Pets are not allowed in evacuation shelters.

If you are staying at home, ride out the hurricane in a safe room. Load up with everything you'll need for 72 hours.

Stay indoors and keep away from windows and doors. Keep flashlights and candles in case the power goes out.

▷ *The middle of a hurricane is a calm spot called the eye'.*

The 'eye' seen from space

IF YOU ARE RIDING OUT A HURRICANE

Keep all your windows and doors tightly shut.
Make sure you have plenty of batteries, tinned food and water.
Listen to a battery-powered radio for the latest information.
Only go outside when you are given the official OK that the hurricane is over.

Hurricanes happen between June and October north of the Equator.
South of the Equator, they occur between November and March.

Hurricanes always start at sea.
They then often head towards land.

Anticlockwise hurricane *Clockwise hurricane*

North
South

Equator

FAST FACTS

HOW TO SURVIVE AN EARTHQUAKE

Movements deep inside the Earth cause earthquakes. During an earthquake, the ground shakes violently, roads break up and buildings can collapse.

▷*A powerful quake can demolish a building.*

Stay away from furniture that might fall

If you are at home, stay inside. Take cover under a table or stand in a doorway, or next to an inside wall.

If you are in a school or office, get under a desk. Do not rush for the exits or stairways. Do not get into a lift.

If outside, stay there, but move away from buildings, bridges and power lines. Stay in the open till the shaking stops.

Try to stay calm. Tremours are usually over quickly. Be ready for aftershocks. Listen to the radio for news.

Earthquake damage

AFTER AN EARTHQUAKE

Check yourself for injuries. If you are fine and know how to do first aid, help anyone who is injured. Beware of broken glass. Keep away from all buildings and power lines. Do not use candles, matches or open flames. Gas pipes and power lines are often broken in an earthquake and can start fires. Get an adult to check for fires, and also the gas, electricity and water supplies. If you smell gas, leave the building and get an adult to send for help.

DID YOU KNOW?
The city of Concepcion in Chile was moved 3 m to the west by a massive earthquake in 2010.

The force of an earthquake is measured on the 10-point Richter Scale.
A quake measuring 9 on the scale is ten times more powerful than one measuring 8.

There are around 500,000 earthquakes every year.
But only around 100 cause any sort of damage.

If you live in an earthquake zone, make sure you have a fire extinguisher.

FAST FACTS

HOW TO SURVIVE AN AVALANCHE

An avalanche is a huge mass of snow that surges down a mountain at high speed, burying everything in its path.

1 **Drop your backpack and other gear.** Do not attempt to out-ski or out-run the avalanche. It is faster than you.

2 **Try to stay upright, or on the surface by grabbing a tree or a rock.** If there are no objects, thrust yourself upwards by kicking.

3 **If you are dragged along, try swimming.** If falling head first, try the breaststoke; if feet first, try backstroke.

△ *Skiers are at great risk from avalanches.*

DID YOU KNOW?

The worst avalanches are 1 km wide and roar down mountainsides at speeds of up to 360 km/h.

Avalanches are most likely to occur on steep slopes, after recent heavy snowfalls and on warm afternoons. Always follow avalanche warnings, get advice from someone who knows the mountains and never ski alone or in the back country without a qualified guide.

90% of avalanches are caused by people's movement. If a group of you are skiing together, always space yourselves out. That way, if some of you are caught in an avalanche, the others can dig you out.

Snow stops your voice from carrying. So don't waste energy yelling until rescuers are near.

Rescue dog

△Dogs are often used to find people trapped under avalanches.

IF YOU ARE BURIED BY SNOW

When you stop moving, curl into a ball with your hands in front of your face. Rotate your head to make an air pocket.
To find which way is up, spit into your hands and feel the way the saliva runs.
Push one hand to the surface to attract help, but don't waste energy unless you can see sunlight. Breathe steadily to preserve energy and oxygen.

Avalanches can happen very suddenly

Do not use the telephone during a storm, except for emergencies

HOW TO AVOID BEING STRUCK BY LIGHTNING

Lightning starts when ice crystals in thunder clouds whizz around so fast the clouds begin to crackle. Giant sparks surge between the clouds and the ground.

▷*Lightning is one of the leading weather-related causes of death and injury!*

DID YOU KNOW?

Lightning does often strike the same place twice. The Empire State Building in New York City is struck 20-30 times each year.

Did you know that rubber shoes do nothing to protect you from lightning?

1 **Seek shelter inside a car with the windows up and the doors closed.** Even if the car is hit by lightning, you should still be safe.

2 **Seek shelter inside a building and shut all the doors and windows.** Do not stand by the windows.

3 **Avoid wide-open spaces, hilltops, high ridges and poles.** NEVER stand under trees. Lightning usually strikes the highest object.

Across the planet there are around 100 lightning strikes every second – more than 8 million every day.
John Sullivan, a US park ranger, was struck by lightning seven times and survived them all – a world record.

Lightning bolts can be more than 8 km long.
Lightning can heat the surrounding air by as much as 28,000°C.

▷*Artificial lightning and cascade transformer.*

FAST FACTS

CAN YOU TELL HOW FAR AWAY THE STORM IS?

To work out how far away a storm is, count the seconds between a flash of lightning and the sound of thunder. Divide the number of seconds by three to find out the distance in kilometres.

4 **Stay away from wire fences or metal objects.** Drop and leave any metal items you have on you, such as an umbrella or keys.

5 **If your hair stands on end, you may be about to be struck by lightning.** Immediately drop to your knees and bend over. Do not lie flat.

6 **Wait for the storm to pass completely.** There is still a risk of being struck more than half an hour after the thunder and rain have stopped.

Tornado winds can whizz around at speeds faster than 600 km/h

HOW TO SURVIVE A TORNADO

A tornado is the world's most powerful wind. There is never much warning before a tornado, so it is important to know what to do.

▽ *A tornado is a whirling funnel of air that destroys everything in its path.*

LIFE SAVERS

Most tornadoes happen during thunderstorms – so stay alert.
Choose a safe place in your home, such as a basement, for your tornado shelter.

Tornadoes can be invisible.
A cloud of dust may be the only sign.

The wind may die just before a tornado.
Make sure you have a three-day supply of food, water, a torch and medicines.

▷ *Be sure to keep a well-stocked first aid kit.*

If you are outside or in a mobile home, go to an emergency shelter. Or get inside the basement or hallway of a strong building.

 Stay away from windows and glass doors, and avoid places with large roofs. Get under a desk and hold on tightly.

 If you are in a car, get out and seek shelter in a building. Never try and out-drive a tornado. The wind can change direction and lift up your car.

 If out in the open, move at right angles away from the tornado's path. Lie down in a ditch, and cover your head and neck.

▲ *Tornado damage*

△ *Tornado winds are so powerful they can pick up cars and toss them around like toys.*

AFTER A TORNADO

With your family, see if your neighbours need help. Give first aid or call for help. Use the telephone only for emergency calls. **Do not drink the water if the pipes are damaged.** Return home only when you are sure it is safe. Get an adult to check for gas leaks. If you smell gas, leave the building. **Listen to the radio for the latest information.**

HOW TO SURVIVE A BLIZZARD

A blizzard is a winter storm with strong winds, driving snow and poor visibility. These conditions can be deadly to the unwary traveller. If a blizzard strikes, seek shelter immediately and stay inside until it's passed.

 If you are outside, don't try to travel. Dig a trench in the snow and line it with branches to protect you from the wind.

 Be careful if you are digging in heavy snow not to overtire yourself. Take short breaks when you feel you need them.

 After the blizzard, help the adults check on your neighbours. Make sure they have enough heat, water and food.

IF YOU ARE TRAPPED IN A CAR

Stay put, or you might get lost. Hang something bright on the aerial so you can be found.
Run the engine 10 minutes each hour to keep it working, and keep the window slightly open.

▷ Metal chains on tyres help the car to grip the road in deep snow.

Snow chains

DID YOU KNOW?

In 1978, a truck driver spent six days in his truck after being buried in a snowdrift. He survived by eating snow.

Cold can be a deadly enemy.
Always listen to weather warnings and when you go out dress warmly.

▷ Always carry a shovel for digging yourself out of a drift.

Snow can bury a landscape in hours.
At the start of winter, prepare an emergency blizzard kit, including jumper cables, a windscreen scraper, food, torches, a tow rope and a mobile phone.

Remember, cold air sinks.
So, if you dig a snow shelter, make sure the entrance is lower than where you're sitting.

LIFE SAVERS

OW TO SURVIVE IN THE DESERT

Deserts are dry, harsh environments. Most have scorchingly hot days, while the nights can be very cold.

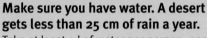

LIFE SAVERS

Make sure you have water. A desert gets less than 25 cm of rain a year. Take at least 4 l of water per person, per day. Make sure your car has spare petrol, spare parts and good maps.

Keep your movements to a minimum. Avoid breaking into a sweat and making yourself dehydrated.

Good sunglasses are vital in the desert.

 Travel at night or early morning when it is cooler. Stay fully clothed during the day to protect you from the sun and prevent water loss.

 Protect your head with a hat or a cloth. Protect your eyes with sunglasses, or rub dirt under your eyes to help cut down on glare.

 Do not ration water. Drink as much as you need. Avoid exercise and have plenty of rest and water - otherwise, you could get heatstroke.

HOW TO FIND
WATER

. . . .

Put a plastic bag over a desert plant and tie closed. In time, water will collect in the bag.
Look for signs of an underground well – you might find one at an old campsite.
If you are short of water, do not eat; the body uses water for digestion.
In the morning, use a cloth to collect dew from the surface of objects (such as metal, leaves and stones) and squeeze into a container.

△ *Cacti contain valuable juices. Cut open the stem and chew, but don't swallow, the flesh.*

Spiny desert cactus

A mirror can be used to signal in the desert

Make use of the car or any natural shelter you can find. If you have to build a shelter, wait until it is cool.

Make shade by building a low wall with rocks or branches. Dig a deep trench on the shady side for you to rest in.

Always tell people where you are going and when you plan to return. They can then search for you if you fail to arrive.

HOW TO SURVIVE AT SEA

It's much more difficult to surive at sea than on dry land. Be prepared for emergencies by taking food supplies and navigation and signalling equipment with you.

DID YOU KNOW?

Raw seabirds are perfectly safe to eat, though they do taste very fishy. Their feathers can be used to make a hat.

△*Life jackets are live savers at sea.*

A buoyancy aid will greatly improve your chances of survival.
Always wear a lifejacket when travelling by boat.

Learn to swim. This is a useful skill whether or not you are at sea.
Being able to swim will make you feel more confident.

Make sure an adult packs an essential items kit.
This should include a first aid kit, water, dry clothes, tinned food, fishing gear, a torch and batteries.

LIFE SAVERS

Hold onto anything that will float. Grab as much material as you can. Try to make a canopy to protect you from the sun, wind and rain.

 If you don't have a lifejacket, a pair of trousers can keep you afloat. Tie the legs together at the ankles, then blow them full of air.

 In the water, your body loses heat quickly. Get out as soon as you can. Use a mirror or flares to signal to any passing boat or plane.

IF YOU ARE ON A
LIFEBOAT

△ *Keep a look out on the horizon for boats that could come and rescue you.*

Stay in the boat for as long as possible. Take whatever supplies you can, especially water and tinned food.
Stay near the place where your boat went down. Rescuers will be looking for you there.
Drink water as you need it. Never drink saltwater or urine. If you are short on water, do not eat.
Keep a lookout for clouds and be ready to catch any rain that falls in shoes, bags and plastic sheets.
Make a fishing line from wire and wood, or from twisted thread. It is safe to eat raw fish. You can fish both day and night.

In the water, keep yourself fully clothed

OW TO SURVIVE ON A DESERTED BEACH

Most beaches offer plenty of resources for an intrepid survivor, with food, fresh water and lots of materials to build a shelter.

 Build your shelter out of the wind and well above the tide line. It's good to build it near food and water supplies, too.

 Build a lean-to frame. Use branches, and thatch it with fronds and leaves. Make twine to tie it together from plant fibres.

 Caves can be good shelters. Build a fire at the back of the cave so that the smoke rises up and drifts out of the front.

To signal for help, light a big fire.
When it is burning well, add green plants on top of your fire to make lots of smoke.

Write a message on the beach.
If your lifeboat is brightly coloured, you could display that, too. Also, use a mirror to flash signals to rescuers.

A good fire can be seen far out at sea.

LIFE SAVERS

A source of fresh water is essential.
First, look for a fresh stream emptying into the sea. If there is one, your job is done for you.

If there is no stream, dig a well above the high tide line. You will probably find water about 1 m down. Boil it before drinking.

Green coconuts contain water.
Bash them against a rock to open them.

Green coconuts

Only eat food that you know to be safe

△ *An unripe green coconut contains about 250 ml (half a pint) of water.*

WHAT TO DO IF YOU ARE CAUGHT IN A FLOOD

After heavy rain or rapid snowmelt, rivers and streams can rise very quickly, and floods can strike with devastating speed.

LIFE SAVERS

Listen to the radio for weather news and leave home immediately if you hear a flash flood warning.
Never cross a flowing stream if the water is above your knees. If you are swept up by the water, grab anything that's floating.

Sandbags can save your home.

1 **If you live in a flood-prone area, always listen out for flood warnings.** Especially in spring, be ready to leave home quickly.

2 **Remember that flash floods are hard to predict.** If it is raining heavily, stay away from streams or dry riverbeds.

3 **Be prepared.** Keep plenty of sandbags. These can keep water out of your home. Keep a supply of tinned food that does not need cooking.

DID YOU KNOW?

Flooding takes more lives and destroys more property than any other kind of disaster.

AFTER THE FLOOD

. . . .

When you return to your home, do not use the lights before the wiring has been checked. Use torches instead. Do not drink water from the tap until you have boiled it for at least 10 minutes. Throw away food that came into contact with the flood water.

△*Never try to drive through a flooded road.*

Just 60 cm of water can carry away a car.

 4 **If the river is rising slowly, help to move animals and vehicles onto higher ground.** Avoid all low-lying areas that might flood.

 5 **Help to lay a wall of sandbags around your home.** You will need to seal any places where water could enter.

 6 **Fill baths, sinks and other containers with fresh water.** You may need it after a flood, as drinking water may become contaminated.

WHAT TO DO IN A FOREST OR BRUSH FIRE

Forest and brush fires start easily when the weather is hot and plants are very dry. In a strong breeze, these fires spread quickly and are a serious threat to people and animals.

▽ *Always make sure camp fires are put out properly.*

Campfire

1 **Be alert: you can often smell a fire before you see it.** Look out for animals acting nervously.

2 **Check the wind direction.** If the wind is blowing towards the fire, move towards the wind; if it's behind it, don't try to outrun it.

3 **Look for a natural break in the trees that would offer little fuel to the fire.** Stay there until the fire has passed.

4 **If you have time, thoroughly wet your clothing.** Then put a damp jacket or hood over your head.

Listen to the radio for fire warnings

IF A FIRE STARTS CLOSE TO YO J

Try, with an adult, to smother it immediately. If you cannot put it out, notify the fire brigade right away. Prepare to leave the area quickly. Make sure your family knows the escape plan. **If you have time, wet your house with a garden hose.**

DID YOU KNOW?

Old campfires can start a fire. When you p   ut a campfire, spread out the embers, pour over water, then top it with dirt.

FAST FACTS

A forest fire can burn an area the size of 400 football fields in just half an hour.
Forest fires advance quickly – as fast as 10 km/h with a following wind.

Lightning bolts are also a major cause of forest fires.
Lightning strikes the Earth more than 100,000 times a day.

Around 5,000 sq km of US forest is burned every year.

HOW TO SURVIVE IN A FROZEN WILDERNESS

For anyone trapped on icy terrain at the North and South Poles, or even on high mountains and glaciers, the extreme cold and biting winds are a severe challenge.

▽ *Wearing the right clothing is vital to protect against cold, wind and glare.*

DID YOU KNOW?

Without clothing, you would survive for just 15 minutes in the Arctic, exposed to −40°C and 50 km/h winds.

1 **Always tell people where you are going and when you plan to return.** Then they'll know where to search for you if you get lost.

2 **Be prepared.** Ensure your parents pack the car with plenty of fuel, spare parts, signalling and navigation kit, tools and a lighter or matches.

3 **Wear several layers of light, warm clothing.** You'll also need a warm hat, a wind-resistant, waterproof jacket and waterproof boots.

Snow and ice cover about 10% of Earth

When cold, your body works harder and needs more food and water. Melt snow and ice over a fire, and boil it in a pan before drinking.

Fish may be your only fresh food. Look for a nearby stream, river or lake.

To catch a fish, use a knife to cut a small hole in the ice, about 30 cm across.

HOW TO MAKE A SHELTER

Build a small shelter out of the wind. It could be a lean-to shelter, a snow trench or snow cave, or a natural shelter such as a tree hollow or rocky cave.

Then build a fire with dry moss, twigs and larger branches. Adding a wall of stones or branches on the opposite side of the fire will help reflect heat back into your shelter.

4 **Tinted goggles protect against the glare of sunlight on snow and ice.** They'll also keep wind, snow and ice out of your eyes.

5 **Unzip or remove a layer of clothes whenever you feel warm.** This will avoid damp, sweaty clothes chilling you later.

6 **Take a warm, waterproof sleeping bag.** This will stop you from freezing at night, when temperatures plunge even lower.

HUMAN HAZARDS

Many of the worst dangers are man-made. House fires, crowd crushes and plane crashes are regular events. To stay safe, it's important to know the safety procedures.

HOW TO ESCAPE FROM A CAR IN WATER

If your car begins to sink in water, try hard not to panic. Panic makes people forget the simplest things and sometimes costs them their lives.

△*In Japan, in 2011 thousands of vehichles were submerged by a tsunami.*

Try to open the windows before the car enters the water. Electric windows will not work once the car is underwater.

Get out while the car is still floating. Use the windows. The doors will not open because water is pushing against them.

If you can't open a window, find something to break the glass. Use your foot if you have to.

No one should ever drive a car over a frozen lake or pond, even if it seems safe. People have often ended up in the water when their car broke through the ice.

A car may float for no more than 30 seconds before sinking

DID YOU KNOW?

All cars will sink in water. The old Volkswagen Beetle is known to float for a few seconds longer than other cars.

IF YOU CAN'T GET OUT OF THE CAR

Try to stay calm. If the car turns upside down, hold onto the steering wheel or a door handle.

When the water level reaches your chin, take a deep breath. By now, you should be able to open a door.

HOW TO AVOID BEING CRUSHED IN A CROWD

Huge crowds gather at street carnivals, sports games and festivals. These events can be a lot of fun, but could lead to a dangerous crush.

1 **If you are being nudged on all four sides, leave immediately.** Make your way diagonally to the edge of the crowd.

2 **If you are caught in a crush, stay calm.** It will help you to find your way out. Stay alert, looking for possible escape routes.

3 **Keep your arms in front of you with your elbows bent, like a boxer.** This will help keep a space for your lungs to breathe.

4 **Keep your legs spread to shoulder-width.** This will help keep you on your feet so that you don't fall and get trampled.

5 **Don't just follow the herd.** This is when a crush can get nasty. People will rush to the main exit, but is there a nearer one?

6 **Never push in a crowd – ever.** Calmly tell people not to push. Project your calm and get people to relax.

Crushes can occur when people are trying to escape from a fire. People panic and bump together and end up moving more slowly, or rush and trample others. Try to remain calm and make an orderly exit from the fire escapes.

FAST FACTS

Most crowd-crush deaths are from suffocation

HOW TO AVOID A CROWD CRUSH

Before going to a big public event, plan where you are going to stand. Some places will be less crowded and easier to leave. Think carefully before getting tickets to events with no seat reservations. Without proper controls, they can be dangerous. If you are standing, stay near the edge of the crowd.

DID YOU KNOW?

A large crowd often acts like a herd. People are so busy following one another that they overlook safe ways out.

HOW TO SURVIVE A PLANE CRASH

It is possible to survive a plane crash. In all but a few accidents, some or all of the passengers survive. As usual, it helps to be prepared and to stay calm.

DID YOU KNOW?

In 2009, a plane leaving New York suddenly lost power. The pilot calmly landed it on the Hudson River, saving all 155 people on board.

Technology makes flying very safe.
The risk of being killed in a plane crash in any year is 1 in 125 million passenger journeys. That's 12 times safer than travelling by car.

▷ *Your seatbelt will secure you against dangerous movement if the plane crashes or stops suddenly.*

FAST FACTS

▷ Read the safety card after the safety demonstration. Read it again before landing.

1 Pull your seatbelt as tight as you can. Bend forward with your hands on your head. Obey the cabin crew's instructions.

2 If you are over water, put on your lifejacket. This is usually under your seat. Do not inflate it until you have left the plane.

3 Move away from any smoke. Try to breathe through a wet towel.

◁ Most commercial airliners are struck by lightning about once a year.

Jets can land with only one working engine

HOW TO ESCAPE FROM A BURNING BUILDING

The key to getting out of a burning building is to know the best escape routes. Be prepared, so you are able to react quickly.

DID YOU KNOW?
Smoke contains poisonous gases, which can be deadly. Most deaths in house fires are caused by breathing in smoke.

 As soon as you hear the smoke alarm, get out fast. Don't waste time saving your belongings.

 If going through smoke, crawl on the ground. The air will be easier to breathe. Cover your nose with a damp cloth.

 Never open a door that is hot to touch. If the door is cool, open it slowly with your shoulder against it.

 If you cannot get out safely, try to go to a room with a window and a telephone. Use tape to seal air vents and doors.

 Call the fire brigade and tell them where you are. Wave something at the window to show them your position.

LIFE SAVERS

Be ready for fire.
Have a smoke alarm on every floor of the house and make sure there is a fire extinguisher, so a fire can be put out quickly.

Make an escape plan.
You need to have two ways to get out of every room. Agree on a meeting place where the family can gather. This way everyone will know that every family member is safe.

Avoid smoke and take the safest route

ONCE YOU ARE OUTSIDE

Call the fire brigade from a neighbour's house.
Never go back into a burning building. Wait for the fire brigade to arrive.

△ *The majority of house fires start in the kitchen.*

HOW TO ESCAPE FROM A SINKING SHIP

Abandoning a ship should be done in an orderly way, but you need to stay calm, think clearly, and move fast.

DID YOU KNOW?

Lifeboats should always stay near a sinking ship. In some past cases, the ship did not sink, and passengers were able to reboard it.

Try not to panic and stay alert. Breathing deeply will help you keep calm. React quickly to any safety annoucements.

Listen for the evacuation signal. This is seven short blasts followed by a long one.

Get into a lifeboat, either on deck or by ladder. Avoid entering the water if possible.

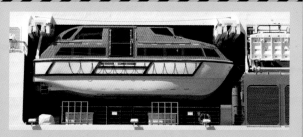

All large ships have lifeboats – small craft that allow passengers to escape in an emergency. Always take part in safety drills, as these will prepare you for a real emergency. Take note of signs in passages and stairways directing you to the lifeboats.

LIFE SAVERS

IF THERE IS AN EMERGENCY

If the ship is listing (leaning over) stay as high as you can and make your way to the deck.

Make sure you've read the safety notices explaining where the lifejackets and lifeboats are kept. If you are below deck, work your way upstairs as quickly as possible.

4 **If there is time, put on as much warm clothing as possible.** Try to cover every part of your body. Fasten your lifejacket securely.

5 **If you are in the water, swim to a lifeboat or a floating object.** Keep as still as possible to prevent losing body heat.

6 **If your lifejacket has a whistle, use it to attract attention.** Get out of the water as soon as possible.

BASIC SURVIVAL SKILLS

This chapter tells you what you need to know, what you need to take and, most importantly, exactly what you need to do when exploring out in the wild.

BEFORE YOU GO ON A TRIP

Make sure you're in good condition and prepare carefully. Taking the right clothes and equipment could save your life!

LIFE SAVERS

Pack some basic kit that might help in an emergency.
A first-aid kit, a small torch and waterproof matches are essential equipment.

△*Bring spare batteries for your torch.*

Take a penknife that has many different tools.
You should also take a whistle, basic cooking equipment and a map of the area you're visiting.

1 Think carefully about what you pack. Pack for the climate and be sure to bring any medications you may need.

2 If you are going somewhere hot, take loose-fitting clothing. Bring a hat, sunglasses and plenty of sunscreen.

3 If going somewhere cold, take warm clothing. Bring a warm hat, socks, boots and a windproof jacket.

TELL SOMEONE

Before you leave, tell someone where you are going.

Then, if something goes wrong, they can send for help.

▷ *A compass is vital in the wilderness.*

Be sure to take insect repellent with you

DID YOU KNOW?

If you have hypothermia, eat high energy food such as chocolate, as it contains lots of fat.

Waterproof matches

LET THE SUN AND STARS HELP YOU FIND YOUR WAY

You don't always need a compass to find the right direction. You can simply use a watch and the Sun or stars to get you on the right track.

USING THE STARS

On clear nights, you can use two star patterns to find your direction.

The two end stars of the Big Dipper constellation in the Northern Hemisphere point towards the bright North Star. North is below this star on the horizon. In the Southern Hemisphere, the two widely spaced stars of the Southern Cross constellation point towards the South. Visit an observatory to find out more.

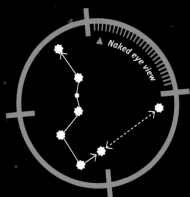

Northern Hemisphere
Ursa Major (Big Dipper)

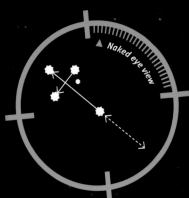

Southern Hemisphere
Crux (Southern Cross)

USING
YOUR WATCH

This works best when the Sun is not directly overhead.

In the Northern Hemisphere, point the hour hand towards the Sun. Imagine a line halfway between the hour hand and 12 o'clock. This line points to the South.

In the Southern Hemisphere, point the 12 o'clock mark towards the Sun. Imagine a line halfway between this mark and the hour hand. This line points to the North.

△*Northern Hemisphere*

▷*Southern Hemisphere*

There are 88 constellations in the sky.
You can see most of them from both the
Northern and Southern Hemispheres,
depending on the time of year.
A few stars are circumpolar stars,
meaning they are visible year-
round from one hemisphere
or the other.

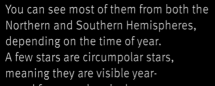

▷*Observatories monitor
the stars. They can give
you lots of information.*

LIFE SAVERS

USING A PENKNIFE

A good penknife will help you to perform all sorts of useful tasks. Keep your knife in good condition, and use it only when an adult is present.

You may need a knife for building a shelter

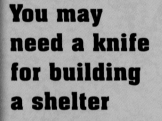

Cutting a branch

▷*Always take care when handling a knife.*

1 **A blunt knife is dangerous and not very useful for cutting.** Use a sharpening stone to keep it sharp.

2 **Lay the edge of the blade against the stone.** Stroke both sides of the blade slowly against the stone.

3 **Use a sweeping motion and continue until the edge is sharp.** Be sure to get an adult to help you.

SAFETY TIP

To open a penknife put your thumbnail in the groove on the knife's blunt side and pull it out as far it will go.

DON'T EXPECT TOO MUCH

It is easier to cut thin strips of wood rather than large chunks. When you have finished, clean your knife and put it away, so you know where it is.

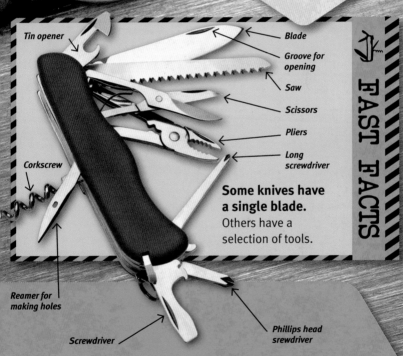

Tin opener

Blade

Groove for opening

Saw

Scissors

Pliers

Long screwdriver

Corkscrew

Some knives have a single blade. Others have a selection of tools.

FAST FACTS

Reamer for making holes

Screwdriver

Phillips head srewdriver

Now wipe the blade up and down against the inside of a leather belt. This smooths and firms the edge.

Once it's sharp, put the blade away. Close a penknife by placing your fingers on the blade's blunt side and gently pushing it.

FINDING WATER

Humans cannot survive long without water. Fortunately, there are many places in the wild where you can find water. Purify any water you collect to make it safe to drink.

Highland stream

1 Wild animals may lead you to water. Fresh water flows in highland streams, which animals drink from.

2 Some plants hold water in their leaves, roots or stems. You can also collect dew from cold surfaces in the early morning.

3 The leaves of fresh, green plants give off water. This can be collected using a plastic bag (see p.39).

Bromeliads hold water

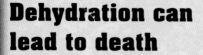

Dehydration can lead to death

Make a rainwater collector by spreading a waterproof sheet on the ground and pegging it with twigs.
Place rocks in the middle of the sheet near the edge and place a container near them.

Make sure the edges of the sheet are off the ground.

Water collects on the sheet and runs into the container.

DID YOU KNOW?

In a cool climate, we need to drink 2-3 litres of water a day. In a hot climate, we need to drink twice as much.

PURIFYING WATER

Water in the wild may contain germs. Always purify water before drinking it.

First, filter water by pouring it through a clean sock or handkerchief lined with a handful of fine sand.
Then boil the filtered water for at least 5 minutes.
When it is cools, store the water in a clean container and keep it in the shade.

MAKING A FIRE

A campfire provides you with heat and light. You can use it to cook your food, purify your water, drive away insects, dry wet clothes – or signal for help. Learn how to make a fire before you travel in the wild.

LOOKING FOR FUEL

Look for the driest kindling you can find, and gather all the fuel you're likely to need before you light your fire.
Tinder (dead moss, leaves, strips of bark) catches fire easily. Fine, dry kindling gets the fire burning, and short sticks will keep it going.

Gather dead leaves for tinder.

Use fine, dry twigs for kindling.

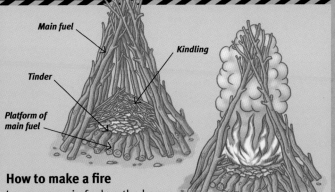

Main fuel

Kindling

Tinder

Platform of main fuel

LIFE SAVERS

How to make a fire

Lay some main fuel on the bare earth. On this platform, place a bundle of tinder and add two handfuls of kindling on top. Place more main fuel around the kindling, making a teepee shape. Then light the tinder.

WARNING!

Keep well away from bushes, undergrowth or hanging trees that could catch light. Build a fire on BARE EARTH or some place where it won't leave scorch marks.

1 **It's great to sleep next to a glowing fire.** To make an all-night fire, arrange the embers of your campfire into a long, narrow line.

2 **Find three logs about 15 cm across.** Place one on each side of the embers, fill the gap with kindling, and put the third log on top.

3 **Build a log or stone 'wall' on the opposite side of the fire.** This will reflect heat back into your shelter while you sleep.

FINDING FOOD

You will probably take food on your trip. But, in an emergency, it is useful to know how to find food in the wild. There is a lot of food you can eat, but do not try anything you don't know. It may be poionous. Only eat foods that you recognize and know to be safe.

DID YOU KNOW?

There are more than 1,400 recorded species of edible insects. Packed with protein, these crunchy snacks are very nutritious.

 To catch a fish, you need a fishing line. You can make a simple line from soaked, braided plant stems or twine.

 Cut a branch about 3 cm long. It needs another branch growing from it to shave into a pointed hook with your knife.

 Cut a notch around the other end. Tie the line tight around the notch. Put live bait (insects, grubs, worms) on the hook.

▽ *Boiled or fried, most insects are safe to eat.*

Fried cockroach

WHICH PLANTS CAN YOU EAT?

Before your trip, find out which edible plants grow in the area: coconuts and plantains in tropical countries, for example, or cranberries, roots and lichens in high mountains.

Blueberries and bilberries grow wild in many places and are good to eat.

Which foods you'll find where depends on the habitat and climate. For example, look for seaweed, crabs and shrimps on the seashore, or water beetles, eels and waterlily tubers in rivers.

The seasons bring different foods, too. In forests and mountains, you'll find berries in summer and nuts in the autumn.

△ *Found on coasts everywhere, seaweed is a popular dish in eastern cuisine.*

▽ *Cloudberries ripen in the summer on far northern highlands.*

◁ *The edible crab is widespread in the northeast Atlantic.*

FAST FACTS

STORING AND COOKING FOOD

Out in the wild, without refrigeration, fresh foods go bad quickly and become breeding grounds for germs. Always cook and eat fresh food quickly, and keep all stored food covered.

KEEPING COOL

In hot weather, keep drinks cool by putting them in a bowl of cold water, or place them in a cool stream, attached by a rope.

Eat all food while it is still very fresh.
Meat, seafood and fish quickly spoil, becoming dangerous to eat.

Preserve extra meat or fish by drying it.
Cut it into thin strips and lay them about 1 m above a smoky fire until dry and brittle.

Dry fruits by slicing them into thin pieces and putting them in the sun. Watch out for bees and other insects attracted to sugary food.

Food can be cooked on heated stones.
Make a bed of large, flat stones. Put tinder and kindling on top and let it burn for half an hour. Brush away the ashes and place the food on top.

You can wrap your food in leaves or put it in a pan.
It will get too hot to touch: remove with tongs or a stick and let it cool before eating.

△*Be careful not to burn yourself.*

LIFE SAVERS

HANGING YOUR FOOD IN A NET PROTECTS IT FROM FLIES

This is vital in the tropics, where flies can carry disease. Make a 'sack' out of fine-mesh net to put around food. Tie the net at the top and hang the larder in the shade.

4 If cooking over a fire, ask an adult for help.
Find a suitable place, avoiding overhanging branches and dry bushes or grass (see p.73).

see p.73

5 Dig out a small trench to make your fire.
When it has burned down to a thick bed of hot embers, you can put a grill over the embers.

6 Find a small green stick and sharpen it at one end. Push small pieces of food onto the stick. Place it over the grill or onto the embers to cook.

MAKING A SHELTER

A small shelter traps heat and keeps out the worst of the weather. In emergencies, knowing how to build a simple shelter can help you survive!

1 To make a triangular frame, tie two short branches to one long branch. Check the frame is wide enough to lie in.

2 Add short branches for the two walls. Make the shelter big enough to cover you, but don't waste energy on making it too big.

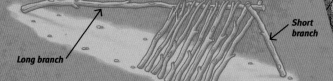

Long branch

Short branch

3 Cover the walls with a layer of leaves, moss and grass. Then add a layer of brush (branches and twigs) to keep the wind out.

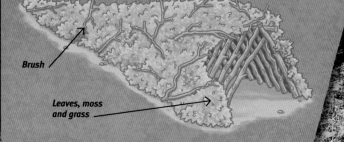

Brush

Leaves, moss and grass

1 **This comfortable bed takes just an hour to make.** Look for logs about 1 m long and 5 cm across, to make your platform.

Platform of dead logs

2 **Drive pegs or stones into the ground at each end, to stop the logs from slipping.** Then add a layer of springy branches on top of the logs.

3 **Cover your "mattress" with softer materials, such as leaves and young branches.** Insulated from the cold ground, you'll get a good night's sleep!

Soft top

Springy branches

Knowing where to build a shelter is just as important as knowing how.

If you plan to stay in your shelter for several nights, make sure you build it near food, a place for making a fire and water.

Or find a natural shelter.

If you don't have time or materials to build a shelter, look for a cave, a clump of bushes, a large, spreading tree or the slope of a hill.

LIFE SAVERS

ANIMALS IN THE WILD

When you enter the wilderness, you are entering the world of wild animals. Most animals will stay away from humans. We should try to stay away from them, too.

Every animal leaves its own unique track

READING ANIMAL SIGNS

△ These fresh prints in the snow show that a wolf has passed by recently.

Keep your eyes open for signs of animals.
Signs to look out for include tracks, droppings, scratchings and the remains of meals.
Before visiting an area, learn which large animals are found there and what their tracks look like.

Arctic wolves live in northern Canada and Alaska.

BEWARE THE MOSQUITO

Female mosquitoes suck blood through special mouthparts, and can pass on malaria.

Mosquitoes are a nuisance, and in some places they carry the disease malaria. Unless you are in bear country, use plenty of insect repellent.

If you find yourself caught in a swarm, cover every part of your body and protect your head with a net or clothing. You should check whether you need to take antimalarial medication before visiting certain parts of the world.

Make plenty of noise when you are out walking. Making a noise keeps animals at a safe distance. Remember, they want to avoid you, too.

Wherever you are, learn about the habits of local animals so that you can avoid them. If collecting water from a place where animals drink, be alert.

Wear shoes and keep your legs covered. When you take off your boots at night, cover the openings with a pair of socks.

Beware watering holes where dangerous animals may gather.

LIFE SAVERS

TIME AND WEATHER

In the wild you take more notice of the natural world. Following the movement of shadows helps you keep track of time. Noticing the clouds helps you predict the weather.

Red sky in morning, sailor take warning

MAKING A SUNDIAL

Stand a stick in the ground. On a sunny day, mark the end of the stick's shadow early in the morning. Mark it again at midday, when the Sun is overhead, and in the evening before it sets. Draw a semicircle between the first and last points (usually another stick and a piece of string).

This gives you a "dial" on which to measure time.

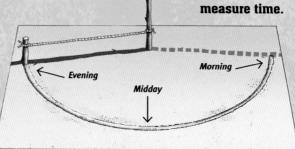

Evening

Midday

Morning

DID YOU KNOW?

If you are shipwrecked, it is important to keep track of the days. Do this by making a mark each day on a rock, tree or stick.

KEEPING OUT THE COLD

If you are unexpectedly caught in very cold weather, stuff your clothes with moss or dry grass. This keeps warm air trapped inside and stops cold air from seeping in. It may feel uncomfortably scratchy, but it could save your life!

Pine cones close when weather is wet.

Predicting the weather helps you to be well prepared.
A change of wind direction or strength may mean a change in the weather.

Watch for natural signs.
Leaves on trees appear to turn upside down when a storm is approaching. Cows sit down when rain is on the way.

Cows ensure they have a patch of dry grass when rain falls.

LIFE SAVERS

GETTING RESCUED

Rescue is the quickest way out of a dangerous situation. Try to get the attention of passing travellers. Thinking of ways to get help gives you less time to worry.

SOS!

In an emergency, you may need to send an 'SOS' ('save our ship') signal.
You can do this in a ground-to-air signal, such as a message in sticks or stones. Make sure that the shape and colour contrasts with the land. Or try using Morse code. In Morse code, the letter S is represented by three dots (short, quick signals), and the letter O by three dashes (long, slow signals). A radio, whistle, puffs of smoke or flashes of light are four ways of sending the signal.

A whistle is a good way of drawing attention if you are lost.

Conserve your torch's batteries. When rescuers are near, signal SOS.

If large enough, your SOS signal will be seen from the air.

Distress signal

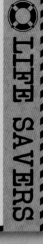

Signalling is a good way of attracting attention.
Choose the best signalling method for your environment. Use sound or light if there is a rescuer nearby to see or hear it.

Make a message using sound.
Blowing a whistle can help alert searchers who are already in earshot. You can also draw attention by shouting.

Make a message using light.
A mirror or a CD is good for signalling in bright sunlight. A flashlight moved from left to right is a good signal. Signal fires that are quick to light may attract a rescue plane. Flares are bright but do not last long. Use them when rescuers are near.

LIFE SAVERS

KEEPING POSITIVE

A positive attitude is very important when you are lost.

It can help you combat fear, pain, hunger and thirst. Stay alert to your surroundings. Keep yourself busy and never lose hope.

If you have a phone, give your location

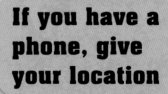

◁Some castaways have been rescued after sealing a message in a bottle and letting the tide carry it away.

GETTING OUT

When you are lost, you have to decide whether to stay put or try to get out. If is usually best to stay where you are and wait till help arrives. If you do have to travel, be very careful.

DID YOU KNOW?
Your body loses heat 25 times faster in water than in air – only enter water if there is no alternative.

Crossing a river by rope

When crossing a river using ropes, cross your feet, and slowly pull yourself across, arm over arm.

Rivers are very dangerous. Only try and cross if you are part of a group.

If in a group, link arms. Place the biggest, strongest person upstream. Cross the river slowly and carefully.

If there are three of you, form a huddle with the strongest person upstream. Stay close together.

The safest method is with ropes and clips. This will stop powerful currents from dragging you under.

LOSING YOUR WAY

· · · · · · · · · · · · · · · · · ·

If you lose your way, stay put until you are rescued. Only set out if you are in danger.

Try to relax and think clearly. Look at your compass. Focus on finding shelter and leaving clues that will make you easier to find.

Don't rush or you may tire yourself out

You stand a better chance of being found if you leave a trail. Mark tree trunks, tie clumps of grass and leave arrows made of pebbles on the ground.

△ *Use stones to show what direction you are heading.*

The easier the route, the better your chances. Try to climb to a high point to examine the land around you. Set a slow steady pace, with plenty of rests.

You can survive for three weeks without food, but just three days without water. Pack plenty of liquid before setting out. And stay dry – your body burns more calories when you are wet and cold.

LIFE SAVERS

FIRST AID

When someone is injured, first aid provides vital relief to stop bleeding, prevent infection and make the person feel comfortable until medical help arrives.

Slide the cloth under the arm to support it.

1 When treating a **BROKEN ARM**, it is important to support the limb. Use a triangular bandage of cloth.

Secure knot at shoulder.

2 Bring one corner around the back of the neck. Then take the opposite corner over the arm to meet it.

3 Tie the ends together. Fold up the third corner of the bandage. Fasten it in place with a safety pin.

Third corner fastened.

1. When treating a BURN, don't apply ice.
Instead place the burn in cool water for at least 10 minutes.

Keep the burn in cool water for 10 minutes.

2. Dry the area gently and protect it with a non-stick pad.
Bandage it lightly, fastening the end with a safety pin.

3. Don't remove anything that is stuck to the burnt skin.
But remove any clothing or jewellery near the burnt area.

Try to keep the burn as clean as possible.

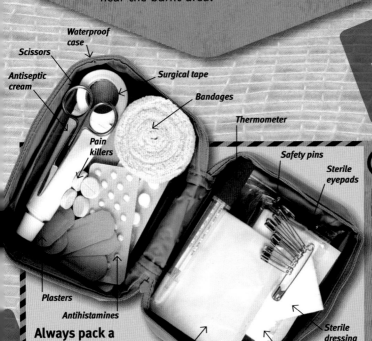

Waterproof case

Scissors

Antiseptic cream

Surgical tape

Bandages

Thermometer

Pain killers

Safety pins

Sterile eyepads

Plasters

Antihistamines

Always pack a first aid kit when you go away.

Antiseptic wipes

Sterile dressing pads

Sterile gloves

LIFE SAVERS

KNOTS

Rope and string are often used to fasten outdoor shelters and make fishing lines or lifelines. Tying good knots is a useful skill.

BOWLINE
.... **Use this knot to make a loop at the end of a rope.**

1 Decide how big the final loop needs to be before you start on the knot – one that can go around your body on a lifeline, for example.

2 To tie the knot, make a small loop over the rope (see above right), then bring the end up through this loop from behind (right).

3 Now take the end around the main rope and bring it back down through the loop.

4 Pull the main rope and the end to tighten the knot. Now you have a loop that will not tighten or slip (though it could come loose if there is no load).

SQUARE KNOT Also called a reef knot.

1 To tie two pieces of rope, cross the right end over and under the left.

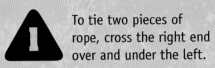

2 Now take the left end and cross it over and under the right. Hold onto both ends.

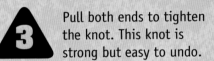

3 Pull both ends to tighten the knot. This knot is strong but easy to undo.

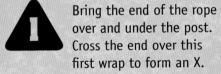

CLOVE HITCH This basic knot ties a rope to a pole or post.

1 Bring the end of the rope over and under the post. Cross the end over this first wrap to form an X.

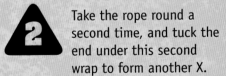

2 Take the rope round a second time, and tuck the end under this second wrap to form another X.

3 Tighten by pulling the end and the main line apart. Use this camping knot to lash your tent to a stake.

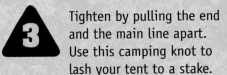

Antibody

A chemical made by the body to fight and kill harmful bacteria, viruses or poisons. Once the antibody has been produced, it stays in the body ready to fight the same germs in the future.

Avalanche

A slide of snow down a mountain slope. Avalanches may be caused by earthquakes, explosions or by the activity of skiers and snowmobiles.

Blizzard

A heavy snow storm with strong winds that can last for many hours. The wind blows the snow horizontally, causing deep snow drifts on the ground and making visibility very poor.

Buoyancy aid (lifejacket)

A close-fitting jacket often made of foam that is worn by canoeists and sailors. If they fall into the water, the buoyancy aid helps to keep them on the surface, but allows enough freedom of movement to swim.

Camouflage

A pattern on many animals' skin or fur that hides them from predators or prey. Some camouflage, such as that of a stick insect, blends the animal in with its surroundings. Other camouflage, such as a tiger's stripes, breaks up the animal's shape to make it harder to spot it from a distance.

Colony

A social group of animals that work closely with each other. Some insects, such as army ants, live in colonies that number several million individuals.

Constellation

An area in the night sky that can be identified by a pattern of bright stars within it. There are 88 official constellations, many of which are based on patterns first identified by the ancient Greeks.

Contamination

The presence of unwanted material or chemicals. It is very important to keep food, water and cooking utensils clean to avoid contamination. Contaminated food or water can spread diseases.

Dehydration

A dangerous loss of water from the body. Symptoms of dehydration include headaches, dizziness and lack of energy. Mild dehydration can be treated by drinking plain water. For severe dehydration, chemicals such as salt also need to be replaced.

Dew

Droplets of water that appear on the surface of leaves and other objects in the morning or evening. Dew is caused when the temperature of the air falls and it cannot hold all the water vapour (the gaseous form of water) in it. The water vapour condenses into liquid water.

Evacuation

The removal of people from an area due to a natural disaster or impending attack. On ships or in planes, the crew are trained in evacuation procedures designed to allow everyone to reach safety as quickly as possible.

Glacier

A slow-moving river of ice that flows slowly down mountains. Most glaciers move about one metre per day, and the ice at the front of the glacier may be several hundred years old. As the ice slides over the ground, it carves out wide 'U'-shaped valleys.

Heatstroke

Illness caused by prolonged exposure to extreme heat. This causes the body temperature to rise to more than 40°C. Symptoms include heavy sweating, rapid breathing and a very fast but weak heartbeat.

Hurricane

A tropical storm with winds in excess of 118 km/h. Also called a typhoon or tropical cyclone, a hurricane can cause waves many metres high and damage to buildings and trees.

Hypothermia

Illness caused by prolonged exposure to extreme cold. The body temperature drops to below 35°C. Symptoms include constant shivering and tiredness. Severe hypothermia can cause death.

Malaria

A disease carried by mosquitoes. It is caused by tiny micro-organisms that enter the blood when a female mosquito bites. Symptoms include headache and fever. Malaria causes about 1 million human deaths every year.

Mangrove swamp

An area of coastal forest where mangrove trees grow in shallow salt water. Mangrove swamps are found in tidal areas in the tropics.

Quicksand

A deceptively soft area that forms when wet sand is suddenly shaken. The sand looks solid, but acts like a liquid as soon as a person stands on it. It is very difficult to escape from quicksand once you are stuck in it.

Suffocation

A lack of oxygen in the body caused by an inability to breathe. It may be caused by choking, drowning or being crushed in a crowd. Suffocation is the main cause of death when large crowds start to panic.

Venom

A harmful chemical that is injected into the body using a bite or a sting. It enters the bloodstream and can cause severe pain or death. Examples of venom include bee stings and snake bites. Venom should not be confused with poison, which enters the body by being eaten or breathed in.

Useful addresses

Scouts

An organisation for boys and girls of all ages providing opportunities for fun, friendship and adventure.
Scout Information Centre, Gilwell Park, Chingford, London E4 7QW
Website: scouts.org.uk

Girlguiding

An organisation for girls where they can have fun, build friendships and make a positive difference to their communities.
The Guide Assosciation,
17–19 Buckingham Palace Road, London SW1W 0PT
Website: www.girlguiding.org.uk

Woodcraft Folk

An organisation providing opportunities for adventures in the countryside for children of all ages from cities.
Units 9/10, 83 Crampton Street, London SE17 3BQ
Website: woodcraft.org.uk

YHA

The Youth Hostelling Association, providing summer activity camps for children. A member of Hostelling International.
Trevelyan House, Dimple Road, Matlock, Derbyshire DE4 3YH
Website: www.yha.org.uk

The Publisher would like to thank the following people for permission to use their photographs (All Shutterstock unless otherwise stated):

Front Cover: Ecelop; 1 Nigel Spiers, 2 Yganko, 3tl 1000 words, 3tr objectsforall, 3b Photoexpert, 4-5 Perrine Doug/Getty Images, 6-7 Sandra van der Steen, 8-9 Tom Reichner, 9tl Maria Dryfhout, 9tr Ria Novosti/SPL, 9b irfanazam, 10-11 Brberrys, 10c Trevor Kelly, 10b Mammut Vision, 12-13 Mike Parry/Minden Images/FLPA, 13t BW Folsom, 13b Jim Agronick, 14-15 Paul Sawer/FLPA, 14 Jochen Tack/Imagebroker/FLPA, 16-17 Theo Allofs/Minden Pictures/FLPA, 16 trekandshoot, 18-19 H&H – J Koch/animalaffairs.com/FLPA, 19t, 19b Peter Waters, 20-21 Peter Davey/FLPA, 20, 21 Mark Moffett/Minden Pictures/FLPA, 22-23 Corbis, 24-25 Anneka, 25 Denis Nata, 26-27 Corbis, 27t NASA, 28-29 Robert Paul van Beets, 29t Pavel L Photo and Video, 29b Maria Suleymenova, 30-31 Andrew Arseev, 31 deepspacedave, 32-33 mashurov, 33 Alexander Kuguchin, 34-35 Minerva Studio, 34 Jojje, 35 Martin Haas, 36-37 Robsonphoto, 37t Wenk Marcel, 37b Michael Dechev, 38-39 Galyna Andrushko, 38 jvinasd, 39 Movementway/Imagebroker/FLPA, 40-41 holbox, 40 objectsforall, 42-43 Pablo Scapinachis, 42 Jason Patrick Ross, 43 Phaitoon Sutunyawatchai, 44-45 riekephotos, 44 ronfromyork, 46-47 Frans Lanting/Frans Lanting Stock/Getty Images, 46 My Good Images, 48-49 Tyler Olson, 48 Yganko, 49 Maksimilian, 50-51 Scott Vickers/Getty Images, 52-53 Yu Lan, 53 Dusaleev Viatcheslav, 54-55 Vladimir Wrangel, 55 Gwoeii, 56-57 Kamenetskiy Konstantin, 56 aslysun, 57 Barone Firenze, 58-59 Gemenacom, 59 tanikewak, 60-61 Adam Bangay, 61 vvoronov, 62-63 Daniel H Bailey/Corbis, 64-65 Sergey Mironov, 64tr Petr Malyshev, 64bl Photoexpert, 65 Andrew Scheck, 66-67 Igor Kovalchuk, 67t KKulikov, 67b holbox, 68-69 windu, 68 Johann Helgason, 69 objectsforall, 70-71 Vladimir Vladimirov/Getty Images, 70t biletskiy, 70b Seth Laster, 71t Marshall Editions, 72-73 Gurgen Bakhshetsyan, 72l Stocksnapper, 72r andersphoto, 74-75 Catalin Petolea, 75t Madlen Shuttersock, 75cl motorolka, 75cr Scisetti Alfio, 75ccr Jiang Hongyan, 75bl Gelpi JM, 75br Madlen, 76-77 Virginija Valatkiene, 77 Charles B Ming Onn, 78-79 Corbis, 80-81 Blazej Lyjak, 80 Critterbiz, 81t Natursports, 81b Arnoud Quanjer, 82-83 Merydolla, 83cl Godunova Tatiana, 83cr Thomas Klee, 83b Corbis, 84-85 Jason Vandehey, 84t optimarc, 84c Li_Al, 84b Nataly Lukhanina, 86-87 grafxart, 86 Oleg Zabielin, 89 Andy Crawford/Getty Images, 90-91 Eugene Sergeev